Totally Bonkers
Music Joke Book

Upbeat Puns & Rhythmic Riddles
To Bring the Giggles Up to Tempo

All rights reserved. No part of this publication may be reproduced, distributed, or transmitted in any form or by any means, including photocopying, recording, or other electronic or mechanical methods, without the prior written permission of the publisher, except in the case of brief quotations embodied in critical reviews and certain other non-commercial uses permitted by copyright law.

© 2022 Jim Chuckles.

This book belongs to

_____

How do you get a standing ovation?

Remove the audience's chairs.

Why led to the singer feeling blue?

A series of ballad decisions.

How are violists' fingers similar to lightning?

They rarely strike the same spot twice.

Why did the pianist bang his head against the keys?

He was playing by ear.

What did the thieves take from the music store?

The lute.

What was Beethoven's favorite fruit?

Ba-na-na-naaa.

What is a golfer's favorite type of music?

Swing.

How do musicians get to gigs on time?

They take the metro-nome.

What's the best present to give a musician?

A broken drum, you just can't beat it.

Did you heard the joke about staccato?

It's too short.

How is a drum solo similar to a sneeze?

You know it's coming but there's nothing you can do to stop it.

Why couldn't the string quartet find the composer?

He was Haydn.

How does a jazz musician end up with a million dollars?

Start with two million dollars.

What type of music do rabbits like?

Hip hop.

Why do drummers keep losing their watches?

Because they have trouble keeping time.

How many conductors does it take to change a light bulb?

One. But it takes four movements.

What is a fish's favorite instrument?

Bass guitar.

How are harps similar to elderly parents?

Both are hard to get in and out of cars.

Why is the pop music industry eco-friendly?

Because they recycle the same four chords.

Who is the favorite singer in Santa's workshop?

Elfis Presley.

What's the difference between an oboe and a bassoon?

You can hit a baseball further with a bassoon.

What musical key do cows sing in?

Beef flat.

What did the piano player say when he had to urgently go to the toilet?

I'll be back in a minuet.

What well-wishes do you send to a music teacher?

Get well tune.

How do you make a French horn?

Stop your car in the middle of the Champs-Élysées.

What do you call a group of killer whales playing music together?

An orca-stra.

Why did the musician hit his rival with a viola?

Because he didn't want to have to resort to violins.

What do you call a guitar player who knows two chords?

A music critic.

What has forty feet and sings?

A choir.

Why did the guitarist lose his job as a carpenter?

Because he was shredding the floors

Why were C, E flat and G told to leave the bar?

Because they don't serve minors.

Why do bagpipers walk when they play?

To get away from the noise.

What is an accordion good for?

Learning how to fold maps.

Which rock group has four guys who can't sing?

Mount Rushmore.

What type of music do wind turbines like?

They are big metal fans.

How can you tell when a drummer is at the door?

The knocking speeds up.

Why are fishermen so good at singing?

Because they can carry a tuna.

How can you tell Mozart was a child prodigy?

All his early works were in A sharp minor.

What is a frisbee player's favorite type of music?

Disco.

Why was the band called 999MB having a tough time?

Because they haven't got a gig yet.

Why didn't Handel go shopping?

Because he was Baroque.

What did the drummer name his twin daughters?

Anna One, Anna Two.

What's the role of a violinist in an orchestra?

To fiddle around.

What happens if you hide a drummer's drumsticks?

He beats his head against the wall.

Why did the pirate learn to play the piccolo?

Because he loved the high Cs.

Musician: Did you hear my last solo?

Friend: I hope so.

What is the loudest pet you can keep?

A trum-pet.

Why were the quavers asked to leave the bar?

Because they were slurring.

Knock, knock.
Who's there?
Benjamin.
Benjamin who?
Benjamin to the music.

How do you show gratitude to the musician playing the triangle in an orchestra?

Thank you for every ting.

How do you hold a Baroque flute?

You Handel it carefully.

What do you call a group of rabbits playing 80s rock?

A hare band.

What do you get when you drop a piano down a mine shaft?

A flat miner.

How are drummers and philosophers similar?

They both perceive time as an abstract concept.

Which is the most musical part of your body?

The nose, because you can blow it and pick it.

Knock, knock.
Who's there?
Turnip.
Turnip, who?
Turnip the music, this is my favorite song!

Why don't basses ever get arrested?

Because they stay out of treble.

Why did the band name themselves Duvet?

They were a cover band.

What is the Earth's favorite musical genre?

World music.

What do a viola and a crime investigation have in common?

Everyone is relieved when the case is closed.

How many altos does it take to change a lightbulb?

None. They can't reach that high.

What is a mummy's favorite type of music?

Wrap.

What do all great composers have in common?

They're all dead.

What is a tornado's favorite song?

The twist.

How do you fix a broken brass instrument?

With a tuba glue.

What's the last thing a drummer says in a band?

Shall we try one of my songs?

What do you call a set of musical dentures?

Falsetto teeth.

Knock, knock.
Who's there?
Sing.
Sing, who?
Whooooo!

Why was the turkey allowed into the band?

It had the drumsticks.

How do you get a three-piece horn section to play in tune?

Get rid of two of them.

What is a composer's favorite childhood game?

Haydn go seek.

What is a skeleton's favorite instrument?

The trom-bone.

How can you tell when a bagpipe is out of tune?

When someone is blowing into it.

Why were flutes invented?

To hit the person on the right.

What's the difference between a viola and a cello?

A cello burns longer.

What happened to the naughty trumpeter?

He was told to stand in the cornet.

What do jazz musicians like for breakfast?

Jam.

Why did the granny sit on her rocking chair with inline skates on?

Because she wanted to rock and roll.

How many drummers does it take to change a lightbulb?

None. There are machines that do that now.

Why did the tortilla chip start dancing?

When they put on the salsa.

How can you tell if a singer is at the door?

They can't find the key and don't know how to come in.

What type of band doesn't play music?

A rubber band.

What's the difference between a rock musician and a jazz musician?

A rock musician plays three chords for 1,000 people and a jazz musician plays 1,000 chords for three people.

What did Beethoven say to Johann when he was parking the car?

Bach it up.

How many bass players does it take to change a lightbulb?

None. The pianist will do it with her left hand.

How do you get two oboes to play a minor second?

Write unison.

Knock, knock.
Who's there?
Little old lady.
Little old lady who?
Amazing, I didn't know you could yodel.

Why were the jazz musicians so busy in the lead up to the concert?

Because preparations were in full swing.

What do you call a musical insect?

A humbug.

What did the drummer say to the bandleader?

Do you want me to play too fast or too slow?

Which classical composer enjoys tea the most?

Chai-kovsky.

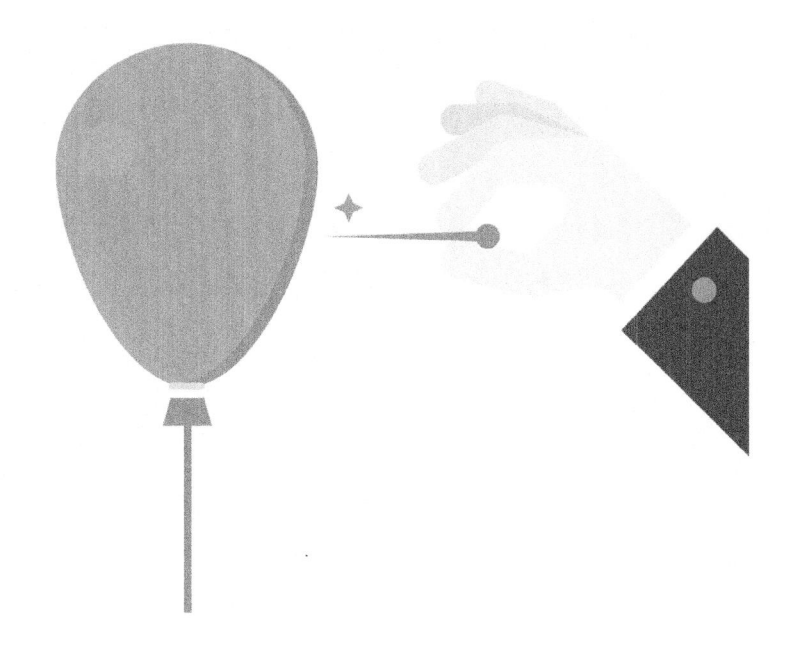

What type of music scares balloons?

Pop music.

How many indie musicians does it take to change a lightbulb?

An obscure number that you probably have never heard of.

♫

What happened after the orchestra was hit by lightning?

Only the conductor died.

♫

Man 1: I lost my entire classical music record collection.

Man 2: Don't worry, I've got your Bach.

What type of music do miners listen to?

Heavy metal.

Why couldn't the athlete listen to music?

She broke the record.

Why can't skeletons play music in church?

Because they don't have any organs.

What did Frédéric do on his day off?

Chopin.

What's the difference between a viola and an onion?

No one cries when you cut up a viola.

Why did the saxophonist take the sheet music home?

So she could practice reeding it.

What musical instrument does a cucumber play?

A pickle-o.

How does a diva sing a scale?

Do, Re, Mi, Me, Me, Me, Me, Me, Me!

Why do DJs make bad fishing buddies?

Because they keep dropping the bass.

What do you call a cow that plays a musical instrument?

A moo-sician.

How do you confuse a drummer?

Give him a sheet of music.

Why is a piano hard to open?

Because the keys are on the inside.

What's the best type of accordion?

A broken one.

What's the difference between a drummer and a savings bond?

One will mature and make money.

What is an avocado's favorite type of music?

Guac and roll.

What happens when you cross a root vegetable with a jazz musician?

A yam session.

What's the definition of perfect pitch?

A throw that lands a bassoon into a dumpster.

What do you call someone who teaches people how to play the French horn?

A tooter.

What type of music does a mountain like?

Rock.

What do you call a gentleman?

Someone who can play the bagpipes but doesn't.

How many sopranos does it take to change a lightbulb?

One. She holds it and the world revolves around her.

Why was the fish so good a playing music?

It knew its scales.

Son: Mom, I want to be a musician when I grow up.

Mom: Sorry son, you can't do both.

What do you call a drummer that loves to box?

A beat-boxer.

What's the difference between a trumpeter's locker and an Englishman?

One has key and trumpets and the other has tea and crumpets.

Did you hear the joke about fermata?

It's a bit long.

Why did the army choir sound terrible?

They had A flat major.

How do you prevent a violin from being stolen?

Keep it in a viola case.

What do you call a bird that forgot the lyrics to a song?

A hummingbird.

What do you call a musician who sings while drinking soda?

A pop singer.

What do a knife and a piano have in common?

They can both be sharp.

Why did the chicken cross the street?

To escape from the trombone recital.

What is a cat's favorite class in school?

Mew-sic.

Why are drummers so impulsive?

Because they never think about the repercussions.

Which type of music is the most hygienic?

Soap opera.

What happens when a piano falls on a trombone?

It will B flat.

Why were the rest of the woodwinds players envious of the flutists?

Because they are the only section members that qualified for the no-bell prize.

What is a planet's favorite type of music?

Nep-tunes.

What's the difference between a drummer and a guitarist?

The drummer has no strings attached.

Why didn't the trumpet player get through the band audition?

He blew it.

Why do fluorescent lights hum?

Because they forgot the words.

Why did the opera singer climb the ladder?

To reach the high notes.

What is an astronaut's favorite genre of music?

Space Rock.

What is a pirate's favorite musical instrument?

A guit-arrrr.

Did you hear the drummer joke?

It's hard to beat.

What do flautists eat for breakfast?

Flute loops.

How can you identify the trombonist's kid at the playground?

It is the kid who is on the slide and can't swing.

How can you tell when a bass player is at the door?

The knocking drags.

What did the hipster put the radio into the refrigerator?

To get cool music.

How do you get a get a trumpet to play forte?

Write mezzo-piano on the sheet music.

Why was there music coming from the photocopying machine?

The paper was jamming.

What do you call a brass instrument that saves money?

A frugal horn.

What is a mermaid's favorite type of music?

The blues.

What did the trombonist show his friends after he returned from his holiday?

A slideshow.

What should you do if you want to sing a song with a friend?

Just duet.

What musical genre do national anthems fall into?

Country music.

MORE FROM THE AUTHOR

1,001 Dad Jokes: Terribly Hilarious Puns, Quips and One-liners

Totally Bonkers Space Joke Book: Humor & Puns That'll Rocket You Out of This World

Totally Bonkers Geography Joke Book: Round-the-World, Geology & Map Jokes To Make You Erupt In Laughter

Totally Bonkers Pilot Joke Book: Silly Aviation Puns, Riddles & Fun

Totally Bonkers Dinosaur Joke Book: "Rawr-some" Fun and "Dino-mite" Laughs

Totally Bonkers Kids Joke Book: 1,001 Funny Riddles, Puns & Laughs

Printed in Great Britain
by Amazon